FLY FISHING ONLY

BY GENE TRUMP

ABENAKI
PUBLISHERS, INC.
P.O. BOX 4100
BENNINGTON, VT O5201

FLY FISHING ONLY

BY GENE TRUMP

Distributed by
THE COUNTRYMAN PRESS, INC.
WOODSTOCK, VT 05091

Published by Abenaki Publishers, Inc.
P.O. Box 4100
Bennington, VT 05201
USA

Distributed by The Countryman Press, Inc.
P.O. Box 175
Woodstock, VT 05091

Printed in the United States of America
October 1993

Cover Artwork by Gene Trump
Cover Design by Todd Horton
Production/Layout Director: Todd Horton
First Edition

ISBN 0-9638388-0-6

Dedicated to the members of the Almost Every Thursday Knights Of The Fly Tying Table, and all the trout who may or may not see the humor in Fly Fishing.

"WELL, YES, YOU'VE CREATED AN INTERESTING BREED OF CHICKEN. BUT I BELIEVE IT'S THE *FEATHERS* THAT FLY TIERS PREFER LONG AND THIN."

"YOUR CHOLESTEROL LEVEL IS FINE BUT YOUR DOUBLE-HAUL NEEDS WORK."

"YOU..AH..EVER USED A FLOAT TUBE BEFORE?"

"THESE BASS SURE HAMMER SURFACE POPPERS!"

"YOU REALLY *GOTTA* WATCH YOUR BACKCAST WITH THOSE *FAST-SINKING* LINES!"

FLY SHOP
FREE CHICKEN DINNER WITH PURCHASE OF #1 DRY FLY NECK.
STONE TRUMP

"YOU'LL FIND WHAT YOU SEEK WITH LONGER LEADERS AND A DRAG-FREE DRIFT."

"FORCEPS!"

"SO...YOU BEEN TRYING THIS SPOT LONG?"

"I SAID *TIE FLIES*... WHEN YOU CAME OVER, I SAID I'D SHOW YOU HOW TO *TIE FLIES!*"

"THEY *RECALLED* MY REEL...!"

"OH, YES, GREAT DYE JOB! BUT WHEN I SUGGESTED YOU BRING ALONG A FEW GREEN DRAKES..."

POTENTIAL PROBLEMS ON THE LOVE BOAT...

"YUP... PAN-SIZE."

"BEST DANGED INSECT REPELLENT I'VE EVER USED! YOU SURE YOU DON'T WANT TO TRY SOME?"

"YOUR SIGN SAYS 'FLY SHOP', SO I JUST ASSUMED..."

"PERHAPS A LITTLE LESS ENTHUSIASM WHEN SETTING THE HOOK?..."

STAND-UP FLY-FISHING COMEDIAN

"SO ONE FLY FISHERMAN SAYS TO THE OTHER: 'WHAT ARE YOU TRYING NOW?' AND THE OTHER SAYS: 'I'M TRYING TO FISH!!!' ...BUT SERIOUSLY FOLKS..."

8.5
9.0
9.0

"OK, WORLD PEACE AND THE END TO ALL DISEASE IS NO PROBLEM— BUT THE BIT ABOUT WADERS THAT NEVER LEAK IS GOING TO BE TOUGH..."

"WELL, YES, AS A MATTER OF FACT I AM A LITTLE NEAR-SIGHTED."

"DON'T WORRY ABOUT IT... I PUT THEM UP MYSELF TO KEEP THE CROWDS DOWN."

"IS IT REALLY NECESSARY TO DANCE A JIG *EVERY* TIME YOU CATCH A FISH?!?"

THE MAILMAN AND THE DOG SALMON

“YEEEEEEHAAAAAAA!”

“SOMETIMES IN LIFE YOU WORK REALLY HARD AND LONG FOR SOMETHING AND SUDDENLY IT'S GONE. BUT TRUST ME, HAROLD, SOMEDAY YOU'LL HOOK ANOTHER FIVE-POUND BROWN TROUT.”

"WOOO-EEE! DID YOU CATCH THE LIGHTNING STORM THAT JUST CAME THROUGH HERE?!?"

"WE SHOULD BE RESCUED ANY DAY NOW! SOMEONE'S BOUND TO FIND THAT NOTE I PUT IN A BOTTLE..."

"I'M REALLY GETTING THE HANG OF THIS CASTING THING NOW."

"...WATERFALLS, FISHERMEN, BEARS...DEATH. I'VE BEEN THINKING IT OVER—YOU GO AHEAD UPSTREAM, I'M BECOMING CELIBATE."

"I REALIZE IT'S ONE HECK OF A HATCH... BUT DON'T YOU THINK WE SHOULD BE GETTING ALONG TO THE CHURCH?..."

"SURE I'VE HEARD OF DUCK CALLS—BUT I DON'T KNOW ABOUT YOUR FISH WHISTLE..."

"CAN WE DO THE MALE-BONDING BIT SOME OTHER TIME? *I'M TRYING TO FISH HERE.*"

"WHEN YOU SUGGESTED TRYING THE GRAVEL BAR...I HAD *NO* IDEA..."

"OKAY, LISTEN UP! CONRAD, COVER THE POCKET WATER DOWNSTREAM. FLEMING, ROLL CAST DOWNSTREAM. TADORAVICH...YOU GO LONG!"

"...PUT UP A HELL OF A FIGHT!"

"I CAN'T UNDERSTAND WHY PEEDEE KEEPS LOSING HIS FEATHERS..."

"NO SIR… EVEN AT THAT PRICE YOU *DON'T* GET THE REST OF THE CHICKEN."

WATER
HAZARDS
GENE TRUMP

"THIS IS ABSOLUTELY THE *LAST* TIME WE SIGN UP FOR THE BUDGET ALASKAN FISHING TRIP!"

ORIGINS OF FLY TYING TERMS: THE WHIP FINISH

GENE TRUMP

"NEVERTHELESS... THE FACT THAT SHE CONSISTENTLY CATCHES FIVE FISH TO YOUR ONE, IS *NOT* GROUNDS FOR DIVORCE."

"FOR CRYING OUT LOUD, HAROLD! AT LEAST WAIT UNTIL I STOP!"

AS NORMAN STEPPED FROM THE TELEPORTER, HE REALIZED THE EXPERIMENT HAD GONE TERRIBLY WRONG.

"IF WE TALK JUST TWO MORE GUYS INTO GOING, THIS ENTIRE TRIP WILL COST US ONLY $1.13 EACH!"

Gene TRUMP

"CARE TO SWIM UPSTREAM TO SEE MY ETCHINGS?"

"SURE YOU NEED TO DRY OUT THE FLY—BUT A COUPLE OF FALSE CASTS IS USUALLY SUFFICIENT."

AS THE STORM RAGED ON, BILL EXPLORED INDOOR ANGLING OPPORTUNITIES.

"PUMPED UP MY WADING SHOES..."

“LAST WARNING, HAROLD—PRACTICE YOUR CASTING ACCURACY *OUTSIDE!*”

"BE THAT AS IT MAY... I DON'T THINK A STONEFLY HATCH JUSTIFIES 120 MILES AN HOUR."

ERNEST PONDERS THE POSSIBILITY OF A MIX-UP WITH HIS VISE ORDER.

"YES, I'M *POSITIVE* IT'S A GRASSHOPPER AND NOT A RATTLESNAKE!"

"I KNOW WHAT THEY *CLAIM* —BUT I'M STILL NOT SURE THEY CLEANED UP THE CHEMICAL SPILL..."

"THAT'S THE BEST STRIKE INDICATOR SYSTEM I'VE SEEN SO FAR!"

Gene TRUMP

"OH... NEVER MIND. NO HATCH. JUST DIRTY GLASSES."

"SOMEONE TOLD HIM THAT A STEELHEAD CAN HIT LIKE A FREIGHT TRAIN."

"HELLO... *NEVER SLIP* WADING BOOT COMPANY?..."

"YEP...THEY DO TEND TO LOWER THIS RESERVOIR'S WATER LEVEL MIGHTY FAST."

"...TWELVE-FOOT LEADER WITH ONE-POUND TIPPET—THEY STILL REJECTED MINE AND TOOK THE NATURALS. SO I TRIED A SIZE 20 EXTENDED-BODY—MORE REJECTIONS. SO I TRIED..."

SMALL BASS OFTEN FALL PREY TO LARGEMOUTHS.

"WELL, WELL, WELL—LOOKS LIKE WE'VE GOT ILLEGAL USE OF LIVE BAIT ON A FLY-FISHING-ONLY STREAM."

INITIALLY, THE DISAGREEMENT OVER THE USE OF NYMPHS VERSUS DRY FLIES SEEMED FRIENDLY ENOUGH...

"I WARNED YOU ABOUT OVER-INFLATING YOUR TUBE."

"DAMMIT HOLMES! I DON'T CARE HOW ELEMENTARY IT IS—TELL ME WHAT THEY'RE TAKING!"

SSSSSSSS
SSSSSSSS

"OF COURSE I MOVED INTO YOUR SPOT—WE'RE CUTTHROAT TROUT FISHING..."

"MANY MOSQUITOES ON THE RIVER?"

"I TOLD YOU IT WOULD BE CROWDED... THAT GUY'S GOT HIS OWN ROCK!"

"MUST HAVE BEEN AN *OLD* FISH..."

"BIG DEAL... HE DOESN'T TELL YOU WHICH FLY TO USE!"

"NEW TO THE FLY-FISHING GAME?"

FLY-FISHING LESSON NUMBER 4: THE REACH CAST

"HOW 'BOUT WE *DON'T* ALL CAST TO THE SAME RISING FISH!!!"

GENE STRUMP

MR. PERRIWINKLE AND THE LEGENDARY CASTING COUCH.

"...I SEE A HUGE CADDIS HATCH. I SEE 20-INCH RAINBOWS FEEDING WITH WILD ABANDON. I SEE MANY FISH CAUGHT. I SEE YOU THERE—A WEEK TOO LATE..."

"GEEZ... THIS SPOT GETS MORE POPULAR EVERY YEAR!"

"OFFHAND I'D SAY HE ISN'T INTO CATCH AND RELEASE..."

GENE TRUMP

"... SO I ASK HIM, 'YOU'RE SURE IT'S SAFE FISHING THIS CLOSE TO THE DAM?' AND HE TELLS ME, 'OF COURSE IT'S SAFE... THEY *NEVER* OPEN THE SPILLWAY WITHOUT GIVING A WARNING.' 'YOU'RE ABSOLUTELY SURE?' I ASKED. 'POSITIVE,' HE SAYS..."

"I THINK THE BEST PART OF FLY FISHING IS THE RELAXATION..."

Gene TRUMP

BRENDA FOUND HERSELF ODDLY ATTRACTED TO THE TALL, DARK STRANGER.

GENE KRUMP

CINDY AND NIGEL, HAPPY WITH THEIR SOLITUDE, WERE TRAGICALLY UNAWARE OF THE IMPENDING INCREASE IN THE NEIGHBORHOOD POPULATION.

ONCE HE STARTED WEARING POLARIZED SUNGLASSES, SID HAD NO TROUBLE SPOTTING ANGLERS.

"NOW WAIT JUST A DOGGONE MINUTE! SOMEBODY HAS JUST SUPER-GLUED A *REAL* MAYFLY ON A BAIT HOOK!"

"YOU KNOW, HAROLD—I DON'T THINK YOU TAKE THIS SPORT SERIOUSLY..."

"HERE'S ANOTHER ONE! AND TO THINK WE'RE USING EXACTLY THE SAME THING AND YOU HAVEN'T HAD A BITE!"

"AS A MATTER OF FACT, NO, YOU *MAY NOT* HAVE A CLOSER LOOK AT MY BAMBOO ROD!"

YOU'RE **SURE** THERE'S GOING TO BE AN EVENING HATCH ?!?

ABSOLUTELY— ANY MINUTE NOW...

“NOPE, CAN’T SAY I’VE HEARD OF A POND SHARK. WHY DO YOU ASK?”

UNFORGETTABLE MOMENTS IN FLY CASTING

DOWSING FOR TROUT

"I CAN'T FIGURE IT OUT... FIRST THE PARTRIDGE FEATHERS. THEN THE MUSKRAT PELT. NOW I'M MISSING A BALL OF YARN!"

"WAITER! THERE'S A WET FLY IN MY DRY MARTINI!"

"WHEN I SAID JUST GIVE IT A GOOD YANK AND IT WOULD BREAK OFF—
I DIDN'T KNOW YOU WERE USING SUCH *&*%#!*! HEAVY LEADER!"

"...SO YOU'VE DECIDED THE BIGGEST FISH ARE ALWAYS CAUGHT BY THE BEST-DRESSED."

HOW TO CATCH FISH
HOW NOT TO BE CAUGHT
GENE TRUMP

About the Author

Gene Trump, whose cartoons have won five Excellence in Craft Awards from the Outdoor Writers Association of America and the Northwest Outdoor Writers Association, is best described in his own words:

"I was born and raised in Oregon's Blue Mountains, where I learned through exposure the ways of the wild and the art of fly fishing. Way too often, I was exposed to yellowjackets, mosquitoes, and statements such as 'they ain't takin' flies.' Driven from the mountains by the recession of '74, I migrated downstream with the best of friends, worst of critics, and the meanest editor I've ever met: my wife Virginia. We took up a feeding station in Corvallis, at the core of the Willamette Valley.

"It was inevitable that I would defy a college advisor who declared I'd never be a writer because I couldn't spell and a high-school art teacher who said my still-lifes were too funny to be taken seriously. I began writing articles and penning cartoons. I may never win a spelling bee, and only the myopic ask me to do their portraits, but *American Angler, Field & Stream, Flyfishing, Fly Fisherman,* and *Gray's Sporting Journal* publish my work regularly.

"My angling motto is, 'Fish have peas for brains, yet we spend scads of time and money convincing them that bits of fuzz and feathers tied to bent pieces of wire are edible. Think about it.' Kind of a long motto, I guess, but fly fishing will always be more enjoyable if you don't take it too seriously. Hence a cartoon book dedicated to that philosophy."